Contents

Introduction

I have struggled with anxiety and worry for quite some time .Thinking to myself the grimly injustice I feel in my heart, seeing and counting all the hurt and pain that I feel inside, listing the names unconsciously of all people and situations that brought me to this gloomy mood. My memory of this cycle spins back to 2009...

For quite some time one would say I have struggled with thoughts of future uncertainties which made me realise as much as I try I was not in control of anything. Managed over the years to convince myself that some level of effort is required in order to eliminate the uncertainties, oh how little did I know and still know.

 If I put some effort it should turn out just fine, the great Rule of life which I had made up in my head went something like this :Cause produces effect and the effect will be what I want and the effect woud be right on time, BOY OH BOY did I have to learn the hard way.
Realizing that my great Rule of life was flawed made me feel this sense of emptiness that drove me to reading a thousand books that warranted how I feel. found myself looking up quotes and scriptures that says you are not crazy and what you are feeling and thinking is real. it was not long, I was calling my one friend who can affirm these feelings and help me be mad at life.

I got gravely sick about how I was feeling, I began to worry and become anxious, angry and suspicious about everything and everyone. I was mad at myself and I convicted myself for anything and everything. I complained a lot probably 23 hours in in a 24 hour day.

It was everyone's faults
Why can't they understand me?
Why can't they see that I need a break?
Why are they so demanding?
Why can't they just leave me alone?
Thought upon, Thought upon, Thought upon, Thought upon, and Thought upon. Am I losing my mind, am I loosing myself? I can't go on like this.

I needed to understand all about life and I remembered reading the phrase "If someone isn't what others want them to be, the others become angry. Everyone seems to have a clear idea of how other people should lead their lives, but none about his or her own." — Paulo Coelho, The Alchemist

AND I WAS THAT PERSON THAT Paulo was talking
about right there, what a revelation, made myself
a cup of tea and decided to meditate about my life
and how I relate to all being in the universe

and

This how im going to deal with myself
Im going to write short poetry and find healing
and
BANG I WROTE

MY HEALING BEGINS
"It's one thing to feel that you are on the right path, but it's
another to think that yours is the only path."
— Paulo Coelho, The Alchemist

Unmasking

I'm going to unmask the person that I am,
Expose myself and hold myself accountable
For this being that I have cultivated for almost 33 years of my
unconscious life.

Of course
I am afraid of being rejected,
Ostracized,
Left-out and
Feeling inadequate
Did you just get that I'm INSECURE, I'm not done
I'm going to unmask the person that I am,
Expose myself and hold myself accountable

See it matters to me that I'm a good person
This view that I hold so dear is merely Selfish
Just To
Escape the wrath of Hell,
Get it, It Gives me the
Feel Good saint Feeling
I surround myself with lots of people
Please them and get my reward the "feel good, saint feeling"
Did you just get that I'm a PLEASER, I'm not done
I'm going to unmask the person that I am,
Expose myself and hold myself accountable

Uhhh the over achieving spirit creeps in
I have to get this,
Do that and
Go there
Completing the to-do list ,
Doing all the rounds gave me the sort of satisfaction
That associated itself with the feel good feeling
Did you just get that I'm IMPRISONED, I'm not done
I'm going to unmask the person that I am,
Expose myself and hold myself accountable

I'm strong,
Intelligent,
I can hold down any conversation and
I'm not weakened by my circumstances
You see it sort of matters quite a lot
to me what people think about me
I'm going to do everything in my control
to make sure that they understand that
I'm strong, intelligent,
I can hold down any conversation and
I'm not weakened by my circumstances
The more they think of me along these lines and
Give me the respect I think I deserve I'm assured the feel good
feeling
Did you just get that I'm CONCEITED, I'm not done

I'm going to unmask the person that I am,
Expose myself and hold myself accountable
But nothing hurts
More than trying to be good and
Strong and
Wise
Deep down knowing that it's weighing you down,

It's probably all for a cause rather than purpose
I'm burnt out,
All out of energy and
full of anxiety and worry simply because
I live for a cause rather than a purpose.
The motives of all my action are selfishly motivated and are
Self-benefiting,
Which screams thoughts in my head of,
If you did it for them then they need to do it for you
Did you just get that I'm FOUL, I'm not done
I'm going to unmask the person that I am,
Expose myself and hold myself accountable

This is ME and
I am Myself
and this is I
My Image is of GOD
He afforded Me
My Will
I WILL different
and YET I AM ME
Will for me
You of THINE Image of ME
Throw Me a Life Line
Did you just get that I'm HUMAN, and I'M Done
I Musk MYSELF IN THINE WILL
Embody ME and I will forever be accountable to Thee

<h1 style="text-align:center">Lifeless</h1>

A Tunnel of life
With No road sign or traffic
The Only Light you have are but your EYES
You think with your SOUL
Yet the consequences of the thoughts manipulate the MIND
You feel mortal and LIFELESS
And Yet the HEART keeps beating the rhythm of life
The tongue along with the lips
Utters words which are familiar to the MIND
But The Heart "dies" not believe
The being is destroyed
For the Air you breath
Is reversed from the corrupted soul into
unbelieving heart
Managed by the manipulated MIND
Living through life LIFELESS
This numb Being needs some resuscitation yall
FREE flow of thoughts through the veins
Rushing to remind the Mind of what the DIVINE planted in your
soul
Of which its real testimony is the beating of the heart to the
rhythm of life

Suddenly the Tunnel of life has a road sign
There is construction ahead read the sign
Peace that surpasses all understating in construction

Immediately your soul is feeding the mind utterance which are
Believable to the heart
The Heart beats faster energetically filling the being with Life
The eyes of the being widens and there is screams
"SHE is alive"
The being is restored
The AIR of the DIVINE breathed into the Mouth
The Spirit of the being mended
Fruits of life and love Refined
Self-Forgiveness
No more condemnation
Righteousness of GOD renewed
Grace become new
Deliverance assured
New Convent established
new life set
A Tunnel of life
With No road sign or traffic
And Yet the HEART keeps beating the rhythm of life
living through life GRATEFUL, PEACEFUL and CONTENT
For MY Lifeless heart, mind and soul has been lifed

Mornings

Morbid ,Stiff
Lead heavy eyelids
Finally opened to meet the sunrise
feet hit the ground
Cold as Ice
A new day has come
meeting it with chores
No time for quite Moments
Mind flashed With TO Dos
Wake them up
Shout to meet times unforgiving orders
It's horns hitting the number hours orderly
Tick , Tick , Tick BOM
BOM my unorganized mind
evoke my mommy mode
Cries, Grovels and screams
Clean Them
Dress Them
Lunch Them
Goodbye Them
as the new day grows old by hours
with old complete routines
Morbid ,Stiff
feather light eyelids
Can't close for a quick prayer
to order the new old days happenings

With Faith
Christians Guilt awakes
Morbid, Stiff push through the feelings
Forget the emotions
Hit the day running
Bath, Dress
Hit the road running
turn the radio Knob
Turn to IMPACT FM
to impact the guilt of the Being
The mornings are harsh
Governed by times horns so ruthless and piercing
will they be forgiving if I start them with
A prayer
Grateful spirit
Praise on my lips
Love in my heart
Peace in my soul
I am a Christian Mom and I struggle with Mornings
Morbid, Stiff giving grey hair to a new born day

Mother's Prayer

The scale of life's happenings
has got me weighty
Pregnant with fear
I need to give birth
Be in labor
Lose some weight
The fruits of my wombs future
Is weighing me down
Got me thinking
I need to pray
Instead
My mind throws petitions
My Fruits future is uncertain
Although the word
tells me not to worry
or be Anxious
The scale of the world's happenings
has me pregnant with fear
Petitions instead of prayers
It hits my soul like
Protect my fruits oh God of My God
Throw them on fertile grounds so they can be fruitful
Water them with THINE Rains so they won't Thirst
Provide them with Wardens that will harvest them with Care
Let them be packaged with their kinds so as not to rot
Deal them to quality markets

let their taste remain sweet
so they bring life to those who Chomp them
fear turned to petitions full of anxiety and worry
I push
I'm in manual labor
My fruits are ripe
Ready and
Able
I'm Weighed down
The Worlds happenings has me pregnant with Fear
Exhausted
fall on my Knees
Let No thorns grow in their Share
Plug off the weeds with your winds
let no birds leave no holes on them
should the above be permitted
Provide them keepers
That will observe their good
Pruning the holes Off so only their finest is left so they can bring
life to those
Who Chomp them
Scale of the world happenings is weighing me down
Knees on the floor
Petitions in my mind
receive them as my prayers my Lord
remaining in You and Thine remain in me
For a branch cannot produce fruit split from the vine
you are the Vine
I remain in you
I produced the fruits of the womb
be their Vine
Amen

Why did I get married?

Subsequent to years of Loves bonds
exchange jewels as a symbol
of the unending merger
Call people to witness
and celebrate
the matrimony of a Marriage
Then why?
Appears like a balanced pace
Subsequent to years of Loves bonds

little did I know
what it takes
full of love for my spouse
Intimate passion ceaseless
Fun galore
Then marriages obligations kicked in
and
Called me Wife
Wife it howled
Let there be a home
Fix meals
keep home tidy
Submit
bear fruits of Thine womb
let there be means in your home
stomach Thine Family's emotions

shoulder their pains
heal their ills and sickness
pledge intimacy with your spouse
Fast for their spirituality
stay on your knees
with petitions to the Divine
And so
Subsequent to years of Loves bonds
MARRIAGE called me by name WIFE

and AS
it appears, I lost my balanced pace
Wiggling around
trying to grip love for balance
fending for fruits of others wombs
respect for fathers I never had until …
with no reverence from them
except when it's for their profit
seeking to take from my fruits' basket
with no mercy
Gained Names behind my back
as they smiled in my face
Marriage called me Wife
and gave me a last name
of many Races and cultures
could not have imagined the
BEARING of the brokenness
to my matrimonial life of a Wife
A fallen Wife
words turned to silence
silence into differences
differences into resentments
resentments into offenses
Heaps of un-forgiveness
Obligations increased
hearts grew cold

Tolerance low
misery Galore
Love leaves here no more
So

Why did I get Married
Appears like a balanced pace
Subsequent to years of Loves bonds
Marriage trembling on the edge
memories of great times lingers
bringing with it hope
remembering connections
Friendship, laughter , Children , Family
inducing Tolerance, Patience, Kindness
and rooting LOVE in My heart
abundant enough to feel it for my husband
and relax me
As a wife in a life of marriage
Why did I get Married
Appears like a balanced pace
Subsequent to years of Loves bonds
I MARRIED FOR LOVE
And MY LOVE IS MY BALANCE
HIS BALANCE IS OUR MARRIAGE
AND so
I CALL MYSELF HIS WIFE

Pain in a Glass

I have rendered my soul
Inhabitable
One glass
one cup
minimized consumption I say
lose focus
lose my mind
body becomes empty as a shell
filled with thoughts and actions
of a bottle
passing false freedom
prisoning those around me
misbehaviors in a bottle
memory loss in a glass
involuntary words in the drink
un-thoughtfulness
Insomnia
sleeplessness

Insomnia
sleeplessness
day dawning
head pounding
hearts broken
Fire water burning my soul
hurt faces

Agony
Broken Promises
Scattered relations
then
memory loss in a glass
what just happened
why so much pain right now
I have rendered my soul
Inhabitable
One glass
one cup
minimized consumption I say

Piercing pain
soul returning to the body
finding shuttered pieces
unable to peace it together
tears
shame
utters of apologies
promises of never again
hope lost in the eyes of the offspring's
shame in my mate's eyes
Scattered relations
what just happened
why so much pain right now
why am I doing this
why do I keep doing It
the freedom that glass promises
the possibilities of a relaxed mind it markets
has me prisoned
in shackles of mountains
of layered
UNEASE
ENXIETY
WORRY

release me
let me go
I belong not unto you
this body is a temple
it houses my soul
my soul houses the HOLY SPIRIT
do not divide me with my divine
be weary O' glass of drink
I'm more than a conquer
I'm the righteousness of God
I'm the daughter of the most high
His Love is mine
My love is his
not one can come in between that
HE will release me
and I will be Free
He will PEACE me together
I will drink from his cup and
I shall never thirst
Your false Promises

I am my mother's child

Memories relived
The eyes that never cried for her husband to be's death
The eyes that never cried when she got stabbed
The eyes that never cried for her premature baby
The eyes that never cried for the beating she has received from a
man
The eyes that never cried for the rape before her offspring's
As I see her betrayed
By another day in this life
Striving to be strong
life dealing her warrior tests
Holding on to her armour
high heels steady
focus never lost
my mind Rewinds
Replays
Repeats
As I demand to forget

Her Strength deceives her
Courage cons her
Her weakness convicts her
Her tears find her guilty and
Announces her weak
Her eyes needed to set her free
Freedom through tears

complete ability to show weakness
But again
Her Strength deceived her
Courage conned her
Her weakness convicted her
Her tears got prisoned in her eyes

She is my mother
I could not have assumed a better mom
I am who I am because she is
she has taught me strength and stillness
Tenacity and Love
her Iron fist directed me
beauty of thousand sun rays
her face still blossoms
she is a women of sixty
and she is my mother
She is fragile Now
she don't need the strength no more
over the years
she depended on Christ
it's who strengthen her she always says

Christ strengthened her she says
Lived within Her
soothed Her
Filled her with hope
and abundance of Love
He would not let her be harmed
He would not permit her to shed a tear
He would not agree her be weary or worried
OH yeah
I get It
she weren't betrayed or desolate
she wasn't trying to be strong
she was a mother

Rested, surrendered in GOD
Filled with strength and stillness
she is a women of sixty
and she is my mother
and I thank God for Her

I feel like writing

L ike exploding from a pen filled ink
Like tearing apart all knowledge that swells
My human brain
Like popcorn in the rain
I am soggy from soaking up pain
I feel like writing
From the depths of my soul
From the pit of my heart
In the
DEEP, DEEP
Dark veins that feed on my emotions
I am confused and I need to release
This beast-like pride
That has captured my pen's glide
Making me hesitant to wriiiite
But
I feel like writing
Like I have the urge to urinate
A river of poetic hate
From past times
And past lines
In dialogue relationships
I just feel like writing to release the negative energy
From current & past enemies
Even in myself
F$%* everybody else

Because
I am my own worst enemy
I just felt like writing.
And so I wrote.

Answered Prayers

L ost within myself
in my space
displaced
misplaced judgments,
complaints
and inadequacies
in awe
In the middle of nowhere
recollection of
God's Generosity
He knew me from my mother's womb
He made plans to prosper me
to die for me
to love me
to provide for my every need
he birthed me, fed me
Provided me with a confident supportive mother
Crazy but always there kind of brother
placed me in a family
to experience his Love
walked with me to school
provided me brains
to absorb and pass all my grades
gave me encouraging friends in my youth
to play with and laugh with

He certified me in higher education
without a cent to loose
permitted me to party and club in dangerous places
without a scar to show for it
gave me a spirit of discernment in my youth
opportunity to learn more about him at the church guild
placed a conscious in me
that has saved my soul so many times
I lost count
because of him
I got my degree
a job
an automobile at the prime of my youth

He afforded me a good man
with a good heart
the one who married me despite all my faults
in the days of my youth
He filled us with dreams
gave us zest for love and life
allowed us fruitful joyous love
and blessed us with the most beautiful
healthy , wise girls of the pack
not only that
might I just say
He knew me from my mother's womb
He made plans to prosper me
he provided us a home
and ensured we sleep with filled stomachs

He sustains me
He keeps me going
he tests me
not more than I can bear
my life is testimony of his very existence
his generosity in My life

is a life of answered prayers
there are tribulations
but he strengthens me
the temptations
but he protect me
there are inadequacies
but he gives me peace
all as he wills
and always on time
I know
because so much generosity
cannot be luck
or coincidence
but a testimony of answered prayers

Heaps of Shit

When the stuffs
people are doing to you
you are already doing to yourself
which grants
those around you
to do to you
what you are
Already doing to
yourself
dammm
woke up feeling this way

You will stop taking advantage of me
because I stopped doing it to me
you will respect me
because I respect me
you will love me
because I love me
you will be accountable for your actions in my life
because I held myself accountable
You will not expose my weaknesses
for I kept yours in heart and secretly helping you with them
you won't deplete my energy with your negative life stories and
expect me to keep my sanity in your presence
That shit is over
Because I ain't taking shit from myself no more

I said
I aint taking shit FOR myself no more
don't invite me to your party
if you aint coming
don't come to my party
if you aint gonna dance to my music
better yet don't bring your playlist to my party
I have got my shit
don't test me
I'm about to fail you

You aint ready to take
What I'm about to dish
I'm pissed you see
not with you
but with myself
I'm demanding you see
of myself
that's which I allowed to be stolen
by my pleasing spirit
I will no longer
take it you see

if you aren't doing to me what I'm doing to me then
get the fuck off my life line
this shit is suffocating
But I'm not about to die
with this pain
I'm gonna release it
till it blows your mind
and you go first
that's how loyal I'm getting
with myself
If this here aint pleasing
then you got the jinx
of what
I'm howling at you

through me
IM OUT

through me
IM OUT

Family matters

family
   we love and live
   but there is thin lines
walked and talked
causing
Harm and Hurt
the stream goes both ways
washing away all the good
making us all the devils' puppets
in our plays
hypocritical statements made
shade everywhere
but still scotching hot
is the pain
Good intentions misplaced
forgetting the binding laws
of
family
Love, teach, guide
for the utmost being to become
heal us oh merciful God
We need your holy intervention
the can be no honor
in children paining the elders
Elders in loathing their children
we are all different

but we of your one image
your image is Love take us back to love and heal my Family

Can I be?

I'm not your sister
I'm not your child
I'm not your daughter
I'm not your mother
I'm not your wife
I'm not your friend
I'm not your colleague
I'm Me
I make my mistake
I Live my life
I love my life
I struggle
I choke
I Rise
I fall
I'm God's
Can I be ?

I cannot be yours
I cannot complete you
I cannot please you
I cannot obey you
I cannot live in your head
I cannot be That for you
That which you
think I must be

I cannot fulfill your Rules
I cannot justify your judgements
I cannot be your hypocrisy
I cannot be your measure of successes
I cannot rectify your own failures
I cannot be punished for your own
I'm God's
Can I be?

I'm conscious of my pain
I'm the assessor of my mistakes
I'm the celebrator of my triumphs
I'm the warrior of my wars
I'm my own worst critic
My own best friend
My own best cheerleader
My best spirit lives in me
It guides me just as yours does you
So I cannot be yours
to mold to your hypocrisy
I'm God's
Can I be

Which God is Yours?

S erving in the presence of my enemies
seeing others cup overflowing
feeling left and forsaken
watching weapons formed against me prospering
running and growing weary
Fruits of my spirit coming rot
with
Envy ....
Jealousy .....
Complete separation from Love
Mentally Unfaithful
Boastful
Loud
Wanting, Needing desperately to know
Which God is Yours
That serves you in the presence of your enemies
while your cup overflows
which God is Yours that
Never leaves you nor forsakes you
which God is Yours That
will never let no weapon formed against you prosper
whom says that you will never run and grow weary
whom keep your spirit fruits from rot
Has you feeling
Content
Love

Kind
Patient
prosperous
I'm wanting , needing desperately to know
For I'm in need of that GOD

Just Thoughts

Through My days
of turbulence and turmoil
I've come to realise
That through saying less
I get to discover who I am
and where I really am going
In contrast to when
I frequently Lash out
Words that really construct this
Fake immoral person I try so hard to Become
I realised a quite person tells
A better version of life
and life to them and those around them
Is a mystery that is so great to unravel
and to you it's like a mission
to find out
what great Happiness being silent really gives me
When I'm silent that the real me
When I talk only God Knows
what I am or
what I have the ability to become
Conceited
Prideful
Immoral
Liar
Deceiver

Jealous or even a murderer
Lest I underestimate the power of the tongue
which manifest itself into my life
Teach my spirit Oh God
To
Look
Listen and
Love

He loved her for himself

As he smiled
laughed daily
held on for dear life
pleaded with life for love
keeping no records of wrongs
lacking pride
Persevering
bounded faithfully

forgotten birthdays
unromantic adoration
no date nights
Overlooked anniversaries
Unbelieve in Valentine's Day
unpacked gifts of love
shallow
but
they mattered to her
rendered her invaluable
unloved
unattended
Unthought-of

As he smiled
laughed daily
hers was loneliness

pretentiousness
powerlessness
Painfulness
Unhappiness in union
simply because
she loved him for him
while to her it appeared
He loved her for himself

the I'm fines that are never probed
smiles unauthenticated
Okays that were never verified
silence that was never examined
sicknesses never taken care of
tiredness that are never heard
hers
pleaded with life for love
keeping no records of wrongs
lacking pride
Persevering
bounded faithfully
while to her it appeared
He loved her for himself

My Africa My soil

I made love with Africa
Now I'm pregnant with pain
I felt South Africa kicking
Telling me how the revolution is eating her young in Southern of Africa
Heard Ethiopia in my fallopian tube screaming how her young never ate last night
I thought of abortion when
The pain of Zimbabwe made me get morning sickness
Wait
I said wait
Is that Nigeria giving me heart burn?
It's that hurt burn from his very soils
His soils that oozes oils
That has the world giving guns to his children
To kill his own born and bred
Wait
I said wait
I'm miscarrying
Blood clots
Blood traces
Blood flowing from Durfur
In Sudan
Call for help, cry for help
Sudan the blood child of Africa
IN floods of blood

About to loose
His children .....
......
Breathe IN and OUT
I'm labour
A whisper in my ear
Complications arise
Push Mother Land
keep pushing
baby cries
Oh South African Child
Born today
Azania is yours
a whisper in my ear
There is a lot blood
there has been a lot of blood
her eyes sight is affected
breath Mother Land
thrash, thrash
baby cries,
breath Mother Land
She is well

I made love with Africa
had my South African child
Born Today
Azania is his

Unimportant wars

S tories in my head
people in my life
Mistakes in my past
uncertainties in my future
unpaid debts
control of my existence
falling of my tears
Desires of my heart
my feelings
myself

Saving others

I see it
I feel it
within me creation of havoc and chaos
Running all day in my mind
Bring my gut into turmoil
My soul into disrepute
Tearing me into pieces
That pain I lash out
Feeling so silenced by the spirit to please
Failing to talk
Failing to say
You hurt me so much and you know it
You did not plan it
But you did hurt me
You are not a bad person
But I feel the pain in my gut
In my mind
In my soul
I see it
I feel it
This pain that is so continuous
Creating within me havoc and chaos
Not sure if I made you do it
Not sure if I'm a bad person
Not sure if I require from you what I don't give
Not sure at all of nothing

Because we never talk about it
Its pain that I lash out
lashing and lashing but never heard
I see it
I feel it
It's just too much to bear
Can we talk about it?
Can we make it right?
When that day comes
May I not be defeated by my spirt to please
for I don't want to please you
I just want to talk about it
And gain myself peace
That surpasses all understanding
For there is a lot of war in the silence
Of the stories we never talk about
Trying to save others

Surviving is not enough

Financially indebted
Emotionally desolate
Spiritually barren
Physically unfit
But I'm surviving
As new days bear sun raise
I'm still here
Breathing
Hanging
Holding
Fighting
Moving
Praying
To do more than survive
To hunt the evil of inadequacy
To Attack it with great enthusiasm
With it lingering
Can I claim to have ever lived?
Surviving is not enough
If you ever had to live
And be alive

Seven Types of hell

Ha! Ha! He! He!
Yah neh
Why would I not identify by them?
Ha! Ha! He! He!
Yah neh
You see you can't speak about it
Till you have been to it
Through it
About it
And almost for it

It's not really tangible you see
It's within and makes you feel without, you see
Ha! Ha! He! He!
Yah neh
It's an inferno
It can't be quenched
Baptism by fire
Scorching every piece of you
You see you can't speak about it
Till you have been to it
Through it
About it
And almost for it

Paul young said

"He joins us in the darkness we create"
Ha! Ha! He! He!
Yah neh
Baptism by fire
Scorching every piece of you
It's within and makes you feel without, you see
Inferno of seven hells:
Unbelieve-Spiritual barrens having no source
Denial - Rejecting to believe truth
Blaming – proclaiming fault unto others
Judgmental - obligating critical point of view unto others
Selfish - fretful principally about oneself
Loveless - inability to give or receive love
Indebted - owing gratitude for a service or favour
You see you can't speak about it
Till you have been to it
Through it
About it
And almost for it
The chronicle of needing
Needing a redeemer
Yah Neh

Lust Languages

How does it work?
How come
Your formulas
Are
Giving
Me
Physiological results
How
Is IT
That
We feel for each other
But
We
Can' be together
How come?
Why ....Mother Nature are u
So
Monogamous
When
It comes to me
Does your formulas
Result
Me
Greedy
To
Want to feel more than once

In One life time
Lust languages

Ultimately

Ultimately what is it all about?
We seek that which we need the most
We become
Grown
Married
Fruitful
Monetarist
Then we stabilize
Then it hit you
You have become but you are not
Not
Happy
Content
Spiritual
Whole
Ultimately what is it all about?
Charity
Giving
Serving
Loving
Could there be no ultimate

Ultimately

____